SPARKLE PRINCESS VS. SUICIDAL PH♥ENIX

SPARKLE PRINCESS VS. SUICIDAL PH♡ENIX

P♡EMS

JEANETTE P♡WERS

Kansas City   Spartan Press   Missouri

Spartan Press
Kansas City, Missouri
spartanpresskc.com

All poems copyright © 2018 Jeanette Powers

First Edition 11 7 5 3 2 1
ISBN: 978-1-946642-81-3
LCCN: 2018964052
Design, Edits and Layout: Jeanette Powers
stubbornmulepress@gmail.com   @novel_cliche
Cover Art and Design: Elim J. Sidus

All rights reserved. No part of this publication may be reproduced or transmitted in any form or by any means, electronic or mechanical, including photocopying, recording or by info retrieval system, w/out prior written permission from the author. Brief passages quoted for review purposes are permitted.

Acknowledgements!
some of these poems have previously appeared in:
Ghost City Press (online August 2018)
Gasconade (2018 NightBallet Press)
The Cosmic Lost & Found
       (2017 Cringe Worthy Poets Collective)
Perfectly Good Muses (2017 Spartan Press)
Tiny Chasm (2016 39 West Press)
Absolute Futility (2013 Write the Future Press)

to those who like to fly blind ...

"You've got to jump off cliffs all the time and
build your wings on the way down."
--Annie Dillard

"Nothing can ever happen twice.
In consequence, the sorry fact is
that we arrive here improvised
and leave without the chance to practice."
--Wislawa Szymborska

The Cosmic Lost & Found

If there's a cosmic lost and found
and you know where to find it
then you know where I'll be:
heaped on top of a pile
of discarded whatevers
lost gloves
and scarves and hats
an inexplicable bathrobe
a number of solo socks
your copy of the Tao te Ching
by Ursula le Guin
the necklace you stole
from your mother
that reminded her
of your father
the keys to the lock
on your glovebox
but not whatever
is trapped in there.

I'm sifting through both
things utterly forgotten and things
that plague you with the nagging

question of where you left them.

I sit on an infinity of bobby pins
and rubber bands
the frame containing
all but the senior year photos
of your son, even the one
where he wore the aubergine beret
there's your ring in the shape
of a leaping horse Nicki lost
there's the leather belt you tooled
in 8th grade shop class with the letters
R O Y, for your grandfather
centered between filigrees
on my lap is the white cat
that ran away one spring
who had white eyes and a fat belly
lying with his head on my knee
is your golden retriever
which your step-father sold
for killing the grass along the fence-line
where he ran and ran.

My bed is made of all the junk mail
never read and never missed
and notebooks lost with only

a few front pages filled with
the insecure marks of hesitant youth
somewhere around here
is your first Danzig cassette
that Bob Dylan poster
and the tape with your father's voice
which you never did listen to
all the way through
because it made you cry so hard to hear.

There I am, adrift
amidst these oddments
the keeper of the left behind
the recorder of what's missing.

There's me whistling
a little tune
you made up
when you were nine
about the clouds
and the horses.

There's me
waiting to be found.

Keep Your Finds

On the ground:
    a rosary.
She thinks:
    no one left this deliberately.

There's a difference between
being lost and being litter.

Was it thrown off in a fit of anger:
    because suddenly God was lost?
Was it dropped in a rush to help a friend:
    because prayers suddenly weren't enough?

In her hands:
    a rosary.
She thinks:
    here is life's great mystery.

We're always wondering
where we came from and why.

We're always left curious
about who lost what and how.

Trinkets

I stole from you.

Trinkets
objects hidden
about your house:
the note I left
behind the painting
your childhood
cricket stick
your Frida lighter
a magnet

minutia

the kind of things
you wouldn't notice
had gone missing
for a long time.

I wanted to take those relics
that you would wonder
when you lost.

I wanted
to be something
you missed

but a small voice
reminded me
that to miss
is also
to never meet
and what if you missed me
in that way?

What if you
never noticed
we trinkets
were gone?

Tree Haus
> —*with Michel Scott*

these falling leaves are just floating perfectly

I think we've talked about how much I love trees
am   in love   with   trees

you dont think i am objectifying them?

I think they consent
also, they are not still life

they are nude

oh no, all that bark is keeping them warm

hmmm

and the sparkle leaves too
warm

trees hardly ever change their minds
trees never move from their homes

and they dont own things
they dont upgrade or diversify

they never speak out of anger
they dont do shame or fear

or talk in tongues
or ridicule
or charge for services
or have small print

I'm feeling your heart so big right now

they mainly just uplift
and dance infinitely slow

and their leaf creaking limb song is a choir

ima build a tree haus
and hardly come down

The Anti-Ego Poem

This is an invisible neck tie party
I model a collar 4 inches wide and 4 inches deep
made of buffalo leather with alligator teeth on the inside
to punish and puncture me with
when I think of doing the things I think of doing
and I have to jerk the chain and say to myself, *bad dog*.

O yes, I have that kind of self-control.
I spent years of self-flagellation
so I wouldn't have to apologize so fucking much
and now I keep that leash real taut
except, except ...

Well you've prolly seen it
I become goddess of the furrowed brow
teeth clench feet tap I try to look relaxed
do that desperate peeping around the room
for someone seeing what I'm seeing
so I can hand the leash to them.

But not a soul, and *wham*
now I'm picking up lost kittens
whose owners are looking for them

and I'm making them mewl for freedom
I'm shoving that baby cat
in the face of the person
telling lies to me and calling it poetry
to show them what honesty sounds like
> *mewl*
>
> *mewl*

this little fur-bag has more guts than you
and now all I want to do is shove it up your ass
till your intestines are lacerations
from a clawing beast who's actually interested in freedom.

"So go ahead and tell me 'bout your bad day!"

Snap. Snap.
Two jerks gets that leash taut
and now I'm sitting
in a peaceful repose
except, except ...

That beautiful girl is throwing herself
at every piece of man-meat
willing to buy her a drink
and begging her to meet his mother
which is what he calls *his cock*
and she's gonna fuck him on Sunday night

because Monday is trash day
and that's where she'll end up
with the shrimp tails
cantaloupe rinds and junk mail.
She'll dig out her new shoes
and wipe the jism off the toes
before stumbling home
so she can wear them next week
singing

"I feel pretty, oh so pretty!"

And I get out the straight razor
catch her on the sidewalk
shave her head, break her mirrors
and wash her face clean
make a fertilizer bomb
and blow up her make-up drawer
her wardrobe and make her
walk naked for three days.

It's too hard to be yourself.
Even I have this collar and leash
because otherwise I'm cliff diving into limestone
toasting to clean living with a bottle of turpentine
rebuilding broken eggshells into whole chickens

and pretending I haven't walked on those eggshells
until my feet were bleeding
and the shells were soft as ancient river stones.
Because I'm always telling myself
to stop talking, to stop spreading my legs
for a certain limp member
being a fling that believes she's loved.

I'm useless as a broken straw
cool as your shirt tucked into your underwear
I have no round squares and I don't believe
I actually exist in the absence of change
and that makes me more masochistic
makes me want claw marks and razor blades
and fertilizer bombs for the cavity
I call my chest, my heart.

Snap. Snap. Snap.
Bad dog.
Relax, baby.
Slow your roll.
Regain the blank slate
except, except ...

I'm hell-bent on headlong
I'm giving myself away like

you're all winners on a game show
parceling out parts of myself

trying to get empty
trying to get empty
trying to get empty
trying to get away
from my self-destructive ways

when I know I was born
to annihilate this life
and what you see today
is a sand castle I built for the beach to see
and the ocean to destroy.

These busy hands are in allegiance
with surviving, not me.

Hence the collar and leash
hence the absence of knives.

except
except
except ...

Snap.

Things I Imagine I Have in Common with Miley Cyrus

The things no one knows
about her are the things
she keeps closest to her chest
they are ornaments of equations
and capital T theories
they shimmer on the tree of her heart
and chime when the cat climbs high in the pine
she is not blonde in the math
of her private places
her tongue only sticks out
to lick stamps there
she is not on stage
but at the desk of her secret mind
and there she finds all the graphs
and calculations that lead to answers.

Deep within Miley Cyrus
is an urge to know why
the diamond began as coal
to know how one proton
separates lead from gold
and it's important to know

her head spins with orbiting planets
it's important no one sees
the experiment her hands compose
figuring how long till the moon drifts away
it's important because if anyone knew
the grand universal longing of her alchemy
her need to be a changeling
her wish to rocket ship away
they would know
the things she doesn't want
anyone to know.

She would become
a public figure
all the way through.

Agitation

@&#^$%
is building frustration
a house of squinting eyes
and worry lines
crossing the face
the world
invading your space
control
faltering
      tectonically
beneath your feet
just before you're grasping
at the broken glass
where the windows
gave way.

Brute momentum
reverberating through your home
and the mounting rage
of treasures taken away
you're shaken and
it's as if someone's
hit the repeat button

on your worst conceptions
the earthquake lasts
a moment
but the agitation remains.

Days, weeks, decades
the anger abides
and cascades
into corners of your mind
long dormant
the dust rising from the basement
the stench of skeletons
fresh again
you can't shake
the wrong done
it shows from the cracks
in the walls
to the pinched lines
between your eyebrows.

Until you can't tell
anyone
whether it's you
or the house
that crumbled
or which is the damaged goods.

Falling Is a Fact

I slip
my feet have
minds of their own
left heading out
and right going home
and what happens
is the same every time
tripping over the same stone
my ass on the ground
and me spilling up
to red-faced stand
looking around
to see who's seen me
as if that'd change
the bruise on my knee
or make me step
more carefully
next time.

Falling is a fact I live with
every tumble inevitable
as getting up again.

Things I Learned from Bill Murray

The first time I saw Ghostbusters, I fell in love ...
with Egon Spengler, because I was a total nerd
and suddenly believed my uber-nerdishness
might someday get me friends like
                Dr. Peter Venkman.

How cool is Peter, right?
I didn't even know what smarmy meant before him.
Turns out it means:
You don't act like a scientist;
you're more like a game show host.

But Bill, I mean Peter,
he kept his cool every minute, I mean,
he sees a 50-story Stay Pufft Marshmallow Man
mangling Manhattan and all he has to say is:
that's something you don't see every day.
No slime, no demon, no gatekeeper, no key-master,
no common decency could ever make Peter break a sweat!
Peter taught us to face our fears
with smug smiles on our faces
and to always cross the streams when duty calls,
and that when you want a dedicated team

of wacky miscreants with
unlicensed nuclear accelerators strapped to their backs,
          who ya gonna call?
Ghostbusters! Classic!

ok. ok ... Caddyshack!
Where we learn that to get a scholarship to college
you have to kiss the ass of a lotta crazy old white men.
You learn you are not supposed
to blast your ghetto blaster
out of your golf bag on the 9th hole.
And now I gotta teach my son what a ghetto blaster is,
          and he also learned
that smokin grass and chasin tail is what adults do
besides taking competition a little too seriously, of course.

But Bill, I mean Carl,
he taught me that it's all right
to want to kill all my toddler's talking stuffed animal toys!
I dynamited that lisping Donald Duck doll,
that cooing Winnie the Pooh,
that freaking Gilbert Gottfried bird!
          ka-boom!
Carl said:
My enemy is an animal, and in order to conquer him,
I have to think like an animal, and

whenever possible, to look like one.
Which is why I wear so much Muppet fur.
So I got that going for me, which is nice.
Now, if Bill gets to be weird as a Tenenbaum,
then go-pher's balls,

                so do I!

And he's got the best movie to teach us how to do that.

Okay, campers, rise and shine
and don't forget your booties
because it's COOOLD out there today!
It's Groundhog Day!

Where we learn finding yourself
is exhausting, mundane, and difficult;
and when everyday looks the same
it ends up feeling
like nothing you do matters.
You can get fat, get laid,
get arrested, kill yourself,
be mean or crude;
and what you find is that the only thing
worth doing on repeat forever is
      learning how to lighten a mood,
      make someone laugh, fall in love,
      and of course,

       save everyone's lives,
because when you can see danger coming,
you're supposed to step up and stop it.

But Bill, I mean Phil Connors,
eventually escaped when he finally found his
       unique, one and only, self.
What Phil let us know,
in the greatest film ever made,
the film the holiday is named after,
what we pay millions of dollars to therapists,
pharmacists and bartenders to find out,

is this:

that you are only gonna be happy
when you find yourself.
And that finding yourself is hard,
takes time, and you are totally
gonna wanna to kill yourself most days.
But when you get it,
that's what they mean by *the sky's the limit*.
And you're gonna start doing it.
After all,
What if there is no tomorrow?
There wasn't one today!

The Smell of Pancakes
—*for my maternal grandfather, Roy Powers*

It was a wonder any of the other cousins
ever got a bite in edge-wise
considering the snake-eye quick-strike
I had when it came to Poppy's pancakes
covered in homemade what-he-called
chocolate gravy.

He stood in baggy, navy blue cut-offs
with a left-over shirt from his Ford days
which still bore an oval patch stitched *Roy*
he meandered the yellow kitchen with Reba-Dog
heelin around on a chance of scraps
over a gas stove with a cast iron pan
he whisked fast at the roilin boil
with those little cocoa chips all we kids snuck
when nobody was sittin or cookin.

The kitchen table always had both leaves in
on account of all the aunts and uncles
dippin in whenever their wallets ran low
or they wanted a night out alone
with the whole mess 'a grandchildren in tow

and it's true that Tammy did paint her name
with fingernail polish into Poppy's el Camino
and it's a fact that Taryn and I filled the whole tub
with his shaving cream though only she got the whippin
because I clung to that kitchen table leg
bawlin until Poppy came to save me and
that's how I learned what *clemency* meant.

Behind the Lazy Susan with Grandma's costume jewels
was the old record player with a radio
and speakers built in
and it played country music or the baseball game
and we grandbabies didn't even know
there were other things in the world
until so much further down the line
and we'd be lonely at breakfast twenty years later
thinking about what we'd rather not have learned.

All the family together wishin just one of us
had learned the recipe for the smell of pancakes.

Coffee at Last
    —for my paternal grandfather, Milford Burns

I never could understand
how when Grandpa's mind went
and gave up his Holy Ghost
to Old-Timers
he was just so
peaceful.

When he'd been such a rush
of business and brutality
and was known for that
through all of his life
when he'd judged so harshly
and baptized so fiercely
and preached damnation
and told me more than once
what waited for me
on the other side of this.

But now, he was just a man
watching his grandson
try to catch hummingbirds
and laughing

passing the casserole
of chicken and rice with peas
and walking the fields
with the family just listening
to everyone tell their tales.

After breakfast was cleared
he and I stayed the table
reading the Sunday paper
with the last of the coffee
he reached over
hand gnarled deep
skin translucent delicate
and gripped my arm
with the strength
of a hard life long lived.

I looked in his eyes
we held the whole of our pain
I think he needed to say
what I needed to hear:

I'm sorry I taught you how to suffer.

All the Balls are in the Air
    --for my son, Elim Sidus

There's no handbook on how make a baby stop crying
and no teacher ever taught you how to placate
an angry husband or a bill collector
or how to stop wishing you'd socked away and saved
that money you spent on another bottle of whiskey
and your friends are all in Vegas for the weekend
and the baby is always the centerpiece
this little raging sunball of energy
this all-consuming spitfire
of tiny toes
and learning to speak
an infinity of dirty diapers, binkies and blankies
you become a professional at naptime
the secretary of bowel movements
overseer of earaches and the absolute dictator
of no-don't-do-that no-don't-touch-that
every second of attention is taken by the child
front and center and in every periphery
you know where every outlet hides
even when she's asleep in your arms
it's part *is she still breathing*
and part *this is the most beautiful being*

and then
you wake up from a particularly deep sleep
the one you've been dreaming of since delivery
and the house is quiet and you snuggle back into bed
for exactly one second before bolting upright
>*why is it quiet?!*

and rushing in to check on the baby
and her crib is plunging soul empty
and your heart buckles in your throat
and you race through the house
and there she is
sitting on the kitchen floor
with the refrigerator door wide open
a dozen broken eggs yellowing
the black and white tiles
and you take a breath
and there's another mess
and she looks up at you and says

>*Mommy, I don't know how to juggle.*

We'll learn, babe, we'll learn.

Fucking Sisyphus

O I'm gonna tell you what really turns me on—
it's someone tapped into the lost art of a lost cause
someone giving up on the whole lousy world
and then choosing to go on
knowing there is no reason to do so
       but the doing.

Fucking Sisyphus, man!
Nothing gets my panties wet like a human
heavy lifting some god-forsaken
boulder up a mountainside besides
watching them chase it down again.

This is not the same as tripping over the same stone.
I like deliberate futility—
going in with eyes unveiled to the purposeless purpose.

Sisyphus had his eyes wide open, he didn't trip or fall
I know. Because if he had I'd been sure
to be underneath him when he did.
His eyes were open, and seeing
he knew his path all too well.

O if you want to woo me, tell me about
your apathy, how you woke this morning
with a choice between a shower and a suicide
              and decided to get clean
opened the windows to let the morning air in
before taking yourself up the hill again—
              and I'm in.

You, shaking your fist at the wind
hollering at the fall leaves falling
putting caterpillars into therapy
telling them ... *you don't have to change*
writing poems on torn napkins
and asking me to stuff those words down my pants
anything useless, outrageous
that asks too much and takes too much
              and I'm all ... blush.

Fucking Sisyphus, man!
That's what I'm thinking about
alone in my bed tonight
with my left hand
between my thighs
and my right hand
      on this pen
getting off on this poem.

Without Knowing

It's knowing
some part of you
still longs for me.

Fall begins
leaves abandon their branches
dry up and break apart beneath our feet
petals crash, spent red and white
against the bare dirt
this drizzle turns to sleet
presently
a reminder of the glacial
pallor your face takes on
when I say *hello*
soon the world will be frozen
soon it will thaw.

I'll never again listen
to the crackling of green shoots
struggling to unearth
the broken leaves
without knowing
that you are listening, too.

Application for a New Muse

Must be willing
to be utterly destroyed
after
tearing down
every wall
and infiltrating
our shared space
so completely
we call ourselves twins
we call ourselves one.

Must be willing to go deeper still.

Must be a reader
no exceptions
no excuses
I mean must legitimately
be obsessed with
and nurtured by
books
preferably sleeps
with one under
your pillow.

Must enjoy secretly watching me
secretly spraying your perfume
into a wad of tissue paper
which I stuff into
my pocket
so
I
can smell
you later
alone.

Must be low-key enchanting
in the way where
your eyes dart after
the first bat
of the night
and dark winds
catch your hair
on the porch step
and when you
share
your two cents
we buy
all the time in the world.

Must be bewitched

with what I create
because you get
that there's really
nothing else
that gets my panties wet
in that
needs to be wrung out
kind of way.

Must have friends
a community
a watering hole
fire pit
must be willing
to kayak down
the Missouri river
by moonlight
with a thunderstorm
on the horizon.

Mustn't be afraid of the dirt of the water.

Must be able to hold my gaze.

Must know how to be silent.
And know when to speak again.

Muse,
> *-for Ezhno Martín*

in the small
of my back
is a pain
where I slept
too long
because
I fell asleep
thinking
of you
next to me
my head
over your
heartbeat
your hand
on my cheek
drifting
away
from the
everyday
impossibilities
and the pain
of old houses

and the songs
once sang
fade away
under closed
eyes
and holding
you close
and being
held
by you
too

I slept
too well
not wanting
to wake up
without you.

Onion Muse
> *--for my mother, Sheri Powers-Cogan*

You are what
is at the bottom
of this crying mess
no one can open you up
without punishment.

You are never simple.

No one really
loves an onion
it's a hard round root
best pureed
powdered
or finely diced
or maybe cubed
but the bigger
the slice of you
the more likely
left on the edge
of the plate
and you feel
how thin

you must be spread
to be palatable.

There is no way
to hold more than
a half dozen onions in one's hands.
Every attempt to embrace
one ends up with a thunk
thunk thunk rolling away.
The onion is combative
anyway, those noxious
fumes payback for being dug up.

Now that we are older
you see we both
don't wrinkle or budge
we rot from within
I eat you like an apple.

Onion Apology

I'm sorry
that you make us all cry
when we think
you are so delicious.

Pickle Muse
> *--for Jayne Montgomery*

I think
you are thinly sliced
and mostly made of water
and vinegar
that
you are a garnish
decorative
and
never the main course.

I love you still.

I sneak you in the afternoon
Gherkin
Bread & Butter
the whole Kosher thing
on the sunny deck
with puppy
dripping brine
and slopping the juice
on my chin.

I pretend you are
a five course meal.

Pickle Apology

I'm sorry I
loosened the lid
and let the air in
when
you were fermenting
all alone so well
sediment
your salt with green
sliced fresh grown earth
sprouted up and cut up
and preserved.

Inside you are thin.
Closed you are untouchable.

Open,
you get eaten whole.

Hokey Pokey Muse

I haven't your knack
for the easy uselessness
I haven't your quack
quack quacking
duck duck goosing
and dodge
ball-games and board games
or how you bend over
backwards to limbo
you are so inbetween
how you right arm in
and then right arm out
as if you were born to it
and jigsaw about as though
your piece fit
every empty slot
all hokey pokey
and London bridges
red rover
you are always sent over
you turn yourself around
and falling down
you are the blackjack dealer

of reindeer games
and I
am red nose
last chose
benchwarmer.

Hokey Pokey Apology

I'm sorry I'm all
ring around the displeases
pocket full of dis-eases
ashes
ashes
I fall right down.

The Muse is Present
> *--for Jason Ryberg*

It's ok to let each other go
because we are never really gone
I can't look at the world
without seeing you in it.

Today, you were the first
green sprig in February
destined to be the little daffodils
and I laughed with you
because of how you always
push through.

Today, you were me
climbing up the steep coast
of the dry creek
with two books in hand
and I didn't fall
because you always
are so sure of where you stand.

And then you were the green briar
I grabbed a handful of inadvertently

to pull myself up over the fallen tree
because of how you bite
when I'm in need.

Now, you are the thorns I pull from my palm.
Now, you are the rustle of the winds lifting
the leaves and hustling them away.
Now you are the slip of blue sky framing
tree branches light with new bud.

Because you are the pain and struggle of creation
because you are the unearthing of a new life
because you are the unreachable horizon
I am forever reaching toward.

Writing Poetry

I'm writing poetry
because staying quiet and doing nothing
is the slow death of stagnation
and even though it frays the nerves
and even though the butterflies in my stomach
have razor blade wings
this poem is what my hands make
of the meteor showers in the night
this poem catches the dust of falling stars
and yes, I'm getting burned
but I'm also passing stardust onto you.

I'm writing poetry because I like doing things
which impress nobody, like letting my toenails grow long
so they cut my lover in bed
or standing outside your doorway
shaking my fist at the wind,
hollering at the fall leaves for falling
putting caterpillars into therapy
and telling them you don't have to change.

I'm writing poetry because
it bursts forth uncontrollably

I'm writing poetry because our dreams
feel so real we think they are until we open our eyes
I'm writing poetry because it's like waking up
and bringing your dreams out with you.

This poem is my best friend
I conjured it up from the best of my most
fanciful imaginings and insurrected
a sidekick in the form of the most abrasive masochist
this side of the seedier side of the gutters of the Orient
this poem is six foot six foot six
and made of circus dicks
this poem is a devil's hodgepodge
of arsenic and laughing gas
this poem is my champion
which protects me when I'm all alone.

I'm writing poetry because
it is the first history of now
archaeologists and historians
will search out these oddments
allegories and eyelashes to figure
what the people were
who we are
this poem is the broken pottery
the monument

the trinket the future has
to remind it of what it doesn't have:
namely you.

I'm writing poetry for you
maybe we are lost at sea being
chased by sharks and hoping for a hurricane
but
I think you are North
I think every compass points to you.

This poem is for you
because your ear is home
because I dreamt you
because by being here
we're both refusing to stay stagnant
we're both refusing to do nothing.

We're looking death in the eye
and saying
this lives on.

Left is Right

Tomorrow I will leave behind
being numb and deaf and blind by choice
tomorrow I will leave behind
not being clear about what I need
of missing the point
of what's going on
of being lazy and boring
first and most
in my own eyes.

Tomorrow I will leave behind
… well …
tomorrow.

I'm going to let tomorrow
be a thing of the past.

Today, I'm full-tilt
all-in
god damn
right now
fuck yes
about time and balls to bones!

I'm gonna leave behind
the immolation
the cell walls
the flagellation
but not
starting tomorrow
starting right (beautiful) now.

I will be never again
I will be punished enough
will be is the wrong tense
I am
done with future fears and past failures.

I will leave behind tomorrow
and yesterday because they can't be grasped
because they aren't real
I was
am
will be am
did do will do
held hold will hold *hello*
now
because this *now*
is the one time
I can have it.

Dear Ms. Atwood,

If you'll excuse me, this isn't a poem
except that this is the way I write when I don't know
exactly how to tell you

stranger

what light of yours has splayed my floors
that I have awoken to
and has caused me to choose to go on

forgive me
I wasn't raised right
instead
I imagined you as my mother
(a once coupling with Vincent van Gogh
               if you were wondering)

and I've stolen from you
as an uncanny teenager might
I've loved you as a tricky mirror

or as a woman whose fingers
are more like redwood trees

than digits
less numerical and more
tangled
blossom
abandon
leave
abandon
begin again
      (you begin this way)

did you ever give up?
(this is a rhetorical question)
did your pen ever fall from your hand
or do you write in pencil?

I scratch out, I do not erase
the terror inside me is that I might forget
or that I might not pay close enough attention
to remember

my books of yours
are cut up like paper dolls
where the dresses are poetry
snippets of poems
and the girl
is me

I'm the letter I send to myself
and the postage due is from you

I arrive home every day

you don't know me
this is melodrama
but in a way
you are saving me from ennui
by existing

you are proof
I have reason

I hope this is no burden to you
but instead, as I mean it
      a *thank you*

you are Helen and Penelope,
waiting and worth fighting for

yours,
Jeanette Powers

Miley Cyrus Makes an Honest Mistake

Miley Cyrus finds herself
in the swimming pool
and the water is sick with chlorine stench
and the children are playing with abandon
which is to her horrendous
and she holds her guts squirming
because her head-ache
is a poltergeist shrieking at the sinking moon
and her stomach is full of butterflies
with chain-saw wings
and she doesn't know why
her body is at war with her
and she doesn't know why
she cannot catch her breath
and she's bobbing in the water
and her heart is exploding in her chest
she knows death is knocking on her rib cage
shaking the bars of her heart to rattle
rattling like the poison and desert snakes
and the children are caterwauling
her throat seizes, she's caught
suddenly the water is too cold
too cold, she will get hypothermia

her body will collapse
all the children will find her dead body
in the deep end, they will dive into her body
lifeless, limp, hair snaking, bloating away
they will have never seen a dead body before
and Miley becomes frightened
she reaches out for a life jacket, bright orange
but grabs a small child instead
she can't see the difference between
innocent life and a life preserver
she carries the child out of the pool
she cannot hear the child screaming
over the lacerating panic in her own head
the child's frenetic kicking
feels only just like her own throbbing heart
the scratching nails are only the pain
of not being, of having never been
she doesn't even exist
she's not even moving away from the pool
she can't even move.

Miley is on the ground
her teeth breathe wet concrete
and ten knees are imprisoning her body
the safety ring flotation device
is moving away in a blur of orange tears

she sees it is not a buoy
it is a little girl.

Grown-ups are weeping and signaling
she can't read lips or braille
she knows that teeth are bared
Miley relaxes into the dark floor
whimpering …

it's me
it's me
it's me

I'm not even here.

The Plan I Made

was to go somewhere
with no point
with nothing
so I threw my belongings
out the second story window
and went downstairs
to see if they had disappeared
but they were just broken
so I made a wish
on the dying body
of my bodily worth
I threw into a fountain
a quarter
I put my car keys
into the hands of a man
wrapped in nothing but a sheet
and got into a white minivan
passing down 39th Street
the driver
platinum blonde
had a voice like reason
and the ass of a goddess
she drove too fast

which I loved
and she stopped for nothing
but the police roadblock
and stashed my stash
in a place it's impolite to look
so I'd be safe going nowhere
she was
on the rag yunno
and as it turns out
a dirty fresh tampon
on the floorboard
of her Windstar
was probable cause
for a strip search
so she bared all
on the side of the road
to distract the cops
long enough
for me to run away
and my last vision
on the path to being lost
on purpose
was her naked body
being ravished
by the men in blue
so I got out the pen

I forgot was in my hair
and wrote her name
across my chest
now my personal space is public
my pockets are empty
I'm off leash
and if you
see me
let me
in
I got nothin
but a handful of it all.

Little Sparkles

There's a little sparkle that lives in my heart
and it shines so quite bright that the inside of my skin
        is prickly sweet like a helium balloon
                filled with orange soda

and that little sparkle inside is what makes me believe
that anything is possible
        like dolphins driving submarines
        playing dominoes with ladybugs
            or bats being afraid of the dark.

I smuggle it fast like a treasure behind my towers
            (an enchanted army)
because the world let me down
so many times
I learned to hide.

Sometimes I close my eyes tight to the world
and pretend all the things I thought as a kid were real:
        and my parents are heroes
        and America is the best thing
        castles are just something for Hobbits
        chess boards, evil queens

and Jimi Hendrix guitar solos.

And everyone has their sparkles shining out
and injustice is only when the dice don't come up right
brutality is the virus killing to live
fight is what we do to cancer
and when all our lights join together

we're stars.

Dear 9 Year Old Jenny Sue,

Remember how today
you realized
that with your imagination you are completely free?
That's not a question, it's a statement!

Remember
how today
you realized
that with your imagination
you
are completely free.

This is the most important moment of your life.
It is the earmark by which you will hear
everything that comes after.
I see you in rainbow suspenders with a book
on the playground and I'm not
going to give you one bit of advice.
I'm not going to school you
or whip you from my 20/20 high-horse.
And the thing about it is:
       you won't let anyone else either!
You are what we politely call strong-willed,

      stubborn
      as a headstrong little girl.

And anyways, Uncle Dwayne already told you:
You ain't like them other cats.
Don't let em scratch it into you.
Little Jenny Sue, you are 9 years old,
and the world is right in front of you.

You are curious as a nine tailed fox
chatting with a fat man under a laurel tree.
You are bright eyed as a first roller coaster ride
carefree as the first green leaf of spring.
You trust the world so much that
you leap off playground swings while blindfolded.
You believe that wings will burst forth
from your shoulder blades and lift you skyward.
You believe the fall won't be fatal
that you will always walk away unharmed.

I bet it's all those books that taught you that!
It's good you love the library.
It's good how you wrap your My Little Ponies
in shoestrings to play Tutankhamun.
It's good you colored the sailboat instead of the butterfly.
It's good you tried to brush the dog's teeth.

It's good you held that dog in your arms when he died.
It's good you cared more for the still living
when your grandfather died.
You are overflowing with love.

You are curious. You ride horses bareback.
You talk to squirrels and they talk back.
They say: *You ain't like them other nuts.*
Don't let em crack you.
And all I really want to say to you is this:

Hey, kid! Keep playing. Keep climbing trees.
Keep inventing constellations.
Keep winking at everyone.
Keep running around naked!
   You're ain't like them other bananas.
   Don't let em peel you.

And they're gonna try to.
They're gonna try to put you in timeout
send you to bed without dinner.

They are gonna try to ground you.

But today, you realized
that with your imagination
   you are completely free.

JEANETTE POWERS IS:

a poet, writer and artist living near the banks of the Gasconade River with their hound dog, Ollymas. Their work has been featured in print and online lit mags, chapbooks (both secret and widely available), and in five previous full-length books of poetry. Their first novella, Victimless Crime, will be released in 2019 by Outlandish Press. Powers has served residencies in St Louis, Missouri; Tuscany, Italy and currently in Belle, Missouri and will be attending Red Gate Residency in Beijing, China in 2019. They founded the indie press, Stubborn Mule Press in 2018, which focuses on first-time full-length books of poetry and collected works from modern greats of indie poetry. Follow them through their website at jeanettepowers.com or @novel_cliche

www.ingramcontent.com/pod-product-compliance
Lightning Source LLC
Chambersburg PA
CBHW030131100526
44591CB00009B/601